PROUSTIENNES

La Presse

PROVIDENCE & PARIS

2016

PROUSTIENNES

BY JEAN FRÉMON TRANSLATED BY
BRIAN EVENSON

Proustiennes by Jean Frémon
Copyright © 2000
Translation Copyright © 2016 Brian Evenson

Published in the United States by La Presse
an imprint of Fence Books

La Presse/Fence Books are distributed by Consortium
www.cbsd.com
www.lapressepoetry.com

Frémon, Jean
Translated from French by Brian Evenson
Proustiennes/Jean Frémon
p.   cm.

ISBN: 978-0-98-643738-0
1. French Poetry. 2. Poetry. 3. Contemporary translation.

First Edition
10 9 8 7 6 5 4 3 2 1

We warmly thank the publishers of the original French editions of
this book, Fata Morgana, 1991, and P.O.L Éditeur, who included it
in *La Vraie nature des ombres*, 2000, for allowing us to publish this
translation.
You can see the complete range of P.O.L's marvelous books at
www.pol-editeur.fr

Proustiennes, understood not as an adjective, which would define a quality, point to a subject, or acknowledge an influence, and which must then apply it—quality, subject, or influence—to something implied by the title, pages, lines, reflections—no. Proustiennes, like Gnossiennes, those lively little melodies by turns solemn or leaping, adventurous, nostalgic, or burlesque, sketches drawn freehand, fearing nothing but heaviness, lightly touching their subjects, approaching them only at an angle, on a tangent, without abstaining from digressions from the path, a trembling and ephemeral shimmer, as from a pocket mirror flashed upon the classroom ceiling to distract the other students and vaguely taunt the teacher or to arrange a rendezvous with an eight-year-old betrothed through a secret, pre-established code. Such lightness can only be applied to a small number of works, those whose particular and universal nature forever shelters them from all pillaging, all treason, and makes every faulty or simply idiotic interpretation harmless and ineffectual. So, with complete freedom, having nothing to convey, nothing to explain, always already poorer, always already nothing, the simple pleasure of strolling at the foot of the Great Pyramid and, as an ordinary tourist, sending a few postcards.

BAD TASTE

The Gnossiennes, whose subtle dissonances seep into the memory more insidiously than many more strongly constructed themes, were composed by Satie in 1890. Who is it who claims that Proust, already enthusiastic about Fauré and Debussy, didn't hear them until, in 1894, the more traditional influence of Reynaldo Hahn encouraged him to take an avid interest in Saint-Saëns's Sonata in *D* Minor for piano and violin, a "mediocre but haunting" melody, says George Painter, "whose only musical merit is its simplicity, and whose fascination comes from its very banality, like that of a popular song or dance-tune." The principal theme of the first movement was to become one of the models for the "little phrase" of Vinteuil's sonata ("to the degree to which reality served me, a very slight degree, to be truthful…"). But Proust is still composing *Pleasures and Days*, in which we find confirmation that he knew Satie's music. In *Social Ambitions and Musical Tastes of Bouvard and Pécuchet*, he imagines that the two Bourdon Boulevard buddies, having exhausted the charms of bicycling and oil painting, diligently apply themselves to music. "But while Pécuchet, an eternal friend of tradition and order, was willing to allow himself be hailed as the last advocate of bawdy songs," Bouvard proves resolutely Wagnerian. And, further on: "Gounod made him laugh and Verdi made him shout.

Less, certainly, than Erik Satie—who could feel otherwise?"
However, doesn't our Bouvard (Wagnerian, like Proust) exert his
eloquence against Saint-Saëns a few lines later, reproaching him
for his old-fashioned approach and his lack of depth? And don't,
incidentally, we see our two arbiters of elegance join together to
lambaste Reynaldo Hahn himself, guilty of liking Massenet?

He also liked the café-concert, Mayol, and Bruant, and it
is with some cunning that Proust, whose tastes resemble Bou-
vard's somewhat, notes in his *In Praise of Bad Music*: "Detest bad
music, but don't dismiss it… Respect for (I don't say love of) bad
music is not simply a form of what could be called the charity
of good taste, or its skepticism; it is also the awareness of the
importance of the social role of music." Let's pass over the social
role, I like *the charity of good taste*, or its skepticism: bad music
is a weakness that you love, like giving in to debauchery; even
when you don't give in to it, your affection for it remains.

OTHER AND SAME

"In every metaphor a little of the magic of being at once alike and different remains," remarks Robert Musil through Ulrich's voice.

"Was it because, having already seen white hawthorn, the sight of a pink hawthorn with blossoms that were multiple rather than singular gave him the simultaneous sense of analogy and difference, both of which have so much power over our minds?" wonders Jean Santeuil, looking for a reason for why he prefers the pink hawthorn to every other flower.

(Philippe Boyer in *Le Petit pan de mur jaune* (*The Little Patch of Yellow Wall*) has skillfully shown how the name of the most common Norman hedge shrub, whose spring efflorescence on the paths of Balbec fills the narrator with so much wonder, plays, through the pun that it contains in French, the role of signaling sexual turmoil.)

Alike or different—papa-mama—chose your team. You're forced to choose, when what you want is nothing but the magic of the both-at-once. Albertine is one metaphor. Agathe is another.

Between these two poles, stretched tight, is fiction. Musil's narrative framework is a net under the feet of that aerialist of thought who successively lets go and grabs hold of the notions which, like heaven-sent trapezes, present themselves to him one after the other, while he measures with irony the gulf that separates the past moment from the future one.

    census of eventualities

    general examination of possibilities

ANALOGY AND DIFFERENCE, AGAIN

The unsaid finds its own path and bursts out sooner or later. Marcel Proust describes an asparagus bed: "the ground was usually quite bare, like the site of all wonders before the magic has done its work, but in June, when he came for Ascension Day, it seemed to Jean's eyes teeming with ten thousand spears of succulent asparagus, thrusting upward, free, as if they weren't, perhaps that very evening, going to be served in his dish, forever uprooted, hot, soft, yet still looking just as he had seen them here. Or, rather, he had seen alive what had been served before him at table: slim, long, some fatter than others, hard and pink, then fading into a faintish blue, with a soft curly green head."

Seven lines farther down, we read: "With every step Jean was brought to a standstill by a fragrant bough, or the upward thrust of a tree in flower, one a simply tasteful ornament, the other a brazen monument spontaneously displayed, or raised aloft, by the spirit of Nature to the Glory of Spring."

The chapter of *Jean Santeuil* in which these lines are found is entitled "The Garden of Forgetting." Memorable forgetting indeed.

TO ACHIEVE HIS ENDS

The dividing line between ambition and a sense of destiny is difficult to establish. But what is an ambition without resources or a destiny that hasn't been lent a hand?

The narrator of *In Search of Lost Time* spends his time postponing his body of work until later, while refusing any commitment (professional ones in particular) that might prevent it from blossoming when the time comes.

Imagine Marcel Proust working until dawn, feeling death prowling around him, and reserving his strength for the development of that idle and weak-willed character that is his narrator. All the work's fiction is in this feature: the incarnation, in the character of the narrator, of the formal structure adopted by deciding to put *Time Regained* at the end of the work and by multiplying the additions—entire volumes—which give its conclusion all its depth.

And however fictive the idler be, he is nonetheless a true and integral part of the worker who shapes him night after night. Like Zhuangzi dreaming of his butterfly, a hard-working writer at his dying breath still dreams that he is a young, idle socialite. Or perhaps it is the reverse.

A young Robert Musil, looking for a place to settle in Berlin, visits rooms—large, small, dark, elegant, or drab—and he writes: "I was looking for something without knowing what: neither an office nor a workroom nor a living room, a room that had been previously inhabited by the man I wanted to become!"

THE SOUL AND THE RADISHES

Washing the first radishes of the year Peter Handke brings them close to his nose to smell their fragrance, which immediately reminds him of the radishes of his childhood. Borges, always in search of new arguments to refute time, obstinately maintains that there is no such thing as the radishes of time past or the radishes of today, that if the smell of one evokes the other it is because they are really the same radishes.

Why am I forced to bring them close to my nose to rediscover the fragrance that I smelled immediately as a child? wonders Peter Handke. That the smell of radishes might be today less strong than yesterday is certain, that my adult sense of smell might have weakened is likely; "everything in that time," he says, "was in its place and I really perceived it, whereas now I need to shift so many things, and they have to wound me for me to perceive them."

But isn't it precisely because everything was in its place then, that it is enough today to displace one component to perceive not the actual smell but what was sleeping within us: a fragrance laden with affect all the more powerful because of that? The mental image of a smell, of which the present radish is in its displacement only an indicator, a mental smell coming from memory that really has very little do with the external sense organs of smell but finds itself directly received by those nerve endings in the brain which are the site of the perception of smells.

Thus, in Proustian terms, this fragrance smelled by Handke would be not the recognition of what is but the resurrection of what we smelled, a fragment of the past that we share.

And what pleases me about this smell is hardly more attached to the radish of today than to the radish of yesterday, but only to the length of time that separates them and that has changed me. Proust refutes our pseudo-Borges. I am touched not by a smell of radishes but by the discovery within me of a distance, of an immaterial depth between the present feeling of what I am and the present feeling of what I was, and I tell myself, there it is, that distance; it's the soul (a word which Musil said that the most remarkable of its properties is really that young people cannot pronounce it without laughing).

TO FINISH OR NOT

The mixed feeling of satisfaction and disappointment upon noticing that things always happen, that what you have most deeply desired, being certain that it was an unapproachable dream, is there before us, and soon already behind.

Madame de Guermantes' invitation to share her box at the *Opera Comique*; Gilberte expressing her pride at being able to say to everyone around her that she is the friend of an author; a book that, if not completed, is at least finally beyond its confused prolegomena, and, in its dimensions and ambition, even stands in for an entire life.

A certain Asian emperor liked construction, architecture, and interior design; he had firm views about the image of himself and of his reign that he intended to leave for posterity through the arrangement of the rooms, hallways, and gardens of his palace. A façade, he knew, is the mirror of its time. And yet he was meticulously careful to staunch the fervor of his architects and interior decorators, and even to disrupt their work with incessant orders and counter-orders so as to be quite certain that the work would never come to an end, that it was always possible to modify, to enhance, to refine that curve, this proportion, that perspective.

Always be very careful not to get caught up in your project, not to be annulled by it. Having devoted your energies to creating an object, be on guard that it doesn't turn against you.

Proust, making from the multiplication of rhymes and echoes a building principle in which reasserting each narrative thread seemingly gives him a second wind, another role to play within a vaster system, opts instinctively for the tactic of the Asian emperor.

Similarly, Musil, sinking into the increasingly more subtle ramifications of the *other state*, did a thing that was wiser than it was immoderate; he preserved his project from an ending which would have been his own end too, and thus was able to die simply, in the course of morning calisthenics.

The main quality of *In Search of Lost Time* is the brilliant insight which closes it, the discovery of *Time Regained*; this marvelous, unstable equilibrium in which the whole is held between two poles, between insouciance and concern, between idleness and hard work, between passion and disillusionment—only the conceptual firmness of the vision of *Time Regained* makes this possible, giving additional meaning, additional necessity, to each episode, to each detail, and to their skillful sequencing. In short, the prime quality of *In Search of Lost Time* is principally that of being a finished, completed book.

The essence of *The Man without Qualities* is, on the contrary, that of being an unfinished, unfinishable book, a book that gets lost in itself.

It is engaged in the portrayal of Ulrich's procrastinations

and moral scruples, his skeptical mind tangling with the grand projects of a waning society, with several eminent representatives coming together within the frame of what comes to be called Parallel Action with the purpose of developing the proper means to celebrate before the world the jubilee of the Austro-Hungarian Empire, which is anticipated—we are in August of 1913—for 1918 (a good part of the irony of the situation and of our complicity with Ulrich, who is the only one to assess it, comes from the fact that we, as readers, know how all this will soon go irreparably out of control). This implacable scorn for all pomposity itself swells up to radically change into a novel of a completely different nature; it is the *other state*, the mystical kingdom, to which the love revealed by his sister Agathe leads Ulrich and which culminates in the constellation of brother and sister: *neither separated nor united*, stealing its end from the satirical story of Parallel Action, all the protagonists of which must, according to the initial plan of the author, meet again in August 1914 for a final session—an involuntary echo of the afternoon party at the Princess of Geurmantes' house, itself a reflection of the evening at Auteuil when the Count of Monte-Cristo takes his final revenge.

Neither separated nor united, but thrown into a scandal beside which Parallel Action is no more than a joke. An unreconciled, irreconcilable story that the author continues to deepen, forbidding himself through this to come to a conclusion.

To finish or not finish a book—which is the positive act,

where does the optimist lie? To finish a book is to accept the idea of writing another. It is to line up thousands of existing books that will be followed by thousands of others. To not finish a book is to pretend to believe that you have all the time in the world to do so. To not stop working on the current book so as to avoid facing the anxiety of the future book is to accept the anxiety of leaving the former unfinished. It is Proust who finds the ideal remedy by giving himself the means to work until his death on an already finished book. After writing *Time Regained*, with failure no longer a possibility, the paperoles[1] could proliferate. If the final meeting of Parallel Action had been written, really written, I mean to say in the novelistic mode, *The Man without Qualities* would be another book, and all the intermediary rough drafts would take on another dimension.

The blunders, the repetitions, the additions imperfectly inserted into the whole, which proliferate in the passages written at the end of the author's life, are in *In Search of Lost Time*, supplementary scintillations, but the real work has been done. How can we not project into our reading what we know of the final days: agitation and nostalgia, passion and disillusionment, time the ally and time the enemy…

In Musil's room on the other hand, is pure serenity; an orderly man who works in the daytime after having surrendered

---

1. The "paperoles" were pages that Proust tore out of notebooks and pasted in to make additions to his manuscript. They sometimes formed scrolls up to two meters long.

himself to his morning exercises, not suspecting that a morning stretch will be fatal for him. The body is not yet aware of the crisis. The fever is there too, but more than the need to finish, to make the episodes converge, is the act of getting bogged down by accuracy. The preliminary draft of the last meeting is deeply moving in that it is so distant from a definitive version. At times, it reminds one of a page from Valéry's notebooks. A last echo of the utopias, "deliver the soul from the weight of civilization," says Agathe. And: "We were love's last true romantics." The notation of detail at the heart of the greatest abstraction, even in the rough draft: "Stumm's face softens, arm movement. The war, old adversary of reverie." It is still the novel, it asks only to remain such, to become such; the ingredients are there, abundant, they collapse together. However, the man of the possible, seated on the bench of the real, has a premonition that soon he will have to stand up.

TO TURN THE PAGE

Proust's acceleration, his racing at the end of each volume (the abominable edition in sixteen volumes, Beckett called it), the way in which, in the final pages, he leaves his subject with lengthening strides. At first you think you've gotten into one of those long, convoluted sentences that come up so often; you are simultaneously happy to have momentarily left the heart of the subject, which was starting to become stifling, and impatient to plunge with restored vigor back into the labyrinths of that all-consuming obsession. But soon you have no choice but to realize that it isn't coming, that it won't come anymore, that the story, like the party, is over. (I use here "story" in the sense of a narrative episode, in the spirit of Mortemart, and not to designate the book in its unity, which is much more than a story.)

Far behind you, as far as the eye can see, is an ocean of oblivion, as if the same phrase which had brought an old business to light with the worry, attention, and anxiety that you know, deposited it again after a long detour on a distant shore, where it seems nothing but a vague memory.

So, *In Search of Lost Time* may also be the story of the narrator's vacillation between absent-mindedness and the most painstaking attention.

"You were saying?... Ah, yes... an old story."

The same thing is, by turns, the object of the wildest obsession and, a moment later, of the greatest detachment.

In *Jean Santeuil* we find an image that foreshadows this movement of acceleration into indifference over what was, not long before, an object of passion. Upon leaving Mass (although a few moments earlier the only permissible greeting was to move over a little to make room in the row for a new arrival), with the stream of the faithful advancing down the center aisle toward the pulpit, Madame Santeuil "said a few words to Madame Savinien, in a voice which she at first kept low, though it grew louder with every step she took, just as a relative gradually but very quickly puts off mourning once the reality of grief has ceased." We pass thus from the confessional to gossip in the church square, and from the consecrated host to the Sunday dinner's cream tart.

TRADITORE

The title *Remembrance of Things Past*, despite having a fully Debussyian harmony and the aura of Shakespeare, doesn't take the ambiguity of Proust's title into account at all. Vanished are: a) the search, b) the loss. The work of idleness, not unlike what others would call the work of grieving.

The time spent losing it. *An evaporated time*, the narrator says, not separate from us, and the entire project consists of finding the catalyst that will permit the operation aimed at condensing this volatile time within himself all over again, then transmuting it into words, into vibrations of words, into processions of words vibrant like the air at ground level under the effect of intense heat, so as to give this mirage material substance again.

Remembrance of Things Past has the merit of trembling like the outline of a jug or bottle painted by Morandi, like the outline of a still-life. It has the breath of life, but can't move. It's a *nature morte*.[2]

And yet it is a quest for the Holy Grail, the *Search!* Vanity, mad ambition, the dimension of the impossible, the title *Remembrance of Things Past* doesn't offer that, it's an elegiac title.

---

2. Trans: The French word for still-life is "nature morte" which literally translates as "dead nature."

Nevertheless, it still has supporters, Keith Waldrop among them. For him, the sense of loss is immediately present if the reader knows the quatrain from Shakespeare.[3]

I had written this after reading—and being enthralled by, since the suppleness of English is suitable for Proust's sentences—the three volume Chatto & Windus edition of the C. K. Scott Montcrieff and Terence Kilmartin translation, purchased in Cambridge on a very sunny day in a beautiful oak-paneled bookstore. My reading began immediately, on a public park bench. I realize today, reading the catalog of Reiner Speck's Proust library, that on the occasion of a new edition done in 1992 the title was changed to *In Search of Lost Time*—a title which Richard Howard just endorsed in a new translation which also changes the famous beginning.

---

3. Trans: From the beginning of Shakespeare's Sonnet XXX: "When to the sessions of sweet silent thought / I summon up remembrance of things past, / I sigh the lack of many a thing I sought, / And with old woes new wail my dear time's waste..."

THE VIEW

Elstir painted not what he knew but what he saw, says the narrator, taking as his own Turner's reply (in an anecdote reported by Ruskin) to a naval officer who asked him why he hadn't pained portholes on his ships.

What is the source of the difference between two paintings of the same object? Between two descriptions of one phenomenon? It's of course that I paint what I see, but I see it only according to what I know, according to who I am, according to what I remember of other objects identical to this one, seen in other times and places and in particular painted by the artists that I like, seeing not through my eyes but through theirs, or by mentally adding mine to theirs, like those old men who, no longer able to focus, sometimes put one pair of glasses over another.

The world exists, but all in all not very much. It is permissible in any case to represent it under its multiple and contradictory forms. Discourse on the little that is reality. To paint chaos, you need a plan. Seeing, knowing, and imagining are equidistant from chaos, any one of them will do. A skillful mixture thickens the stew.

LEITMOTIF

Long phrases that are deployed in successive waves and then withdraw, allowing yawning gaps, abeyances, and overhangs to appear, from which a few musical notes, the most emblematic ones, will be picked up again, here by the soloist, there by the bass, while on the surface a fixed scintillation is deployed similar to light diffracted in the hot air above the ground, later by the entire orchestra in unison, multiple emergences of the leitmotif in the depth of the phrasing—how can we not see in the Wagnerian system an echo not only of Proust's style but of his project itself?

"A mnemonic system," Baudelaire calls the leitmotif. "Each character is, so to speak, branded by the melody that represents his moral character and the role he is called upon to play in the tale." And Baudelaire is not afraid to cite in this connection his *Correspondences* (*Correspondences* was published in 1857, Wagner's first concerts in Paris date from the winter of 1860).

But there is more. When Liszt says of Wagner: "His themes are personifications of ideas," he indicates how, beyond simple designations of characters, a musical motif is charged by the author with being the vector of a sensation, and also how, so as to allow it to be perceived in its variations, he repeats it skillfully transposed in situations that put into play comparable sensations, ideas, and even opinions.

Assonance, the thoroughly musical technique of internal rhyme, starts to echo themes that mutually illuminate and prolong one another, weaving between the past and the present of the fiction those essential links that give the *Search* its internal structure. Just as the story of Swan's jealousy and Odette's thoughtlessness parallels the tormented affair of the narrator and Albertine. Likewise the Dreyfus Affair, a mirror in which the narrator deciphers the symptoms of the evils from which the society that he rubs shoulders with suffers and where the blurred silhouette of the author himself appears and is transposed from the political to the aesthetical, with the same recoiling from the face of what is perceived to be a questioning of institutions and traditions, the same chauvinistic cold feet and the same xenophobic affronts as in the polemics that the introduction of Wagner's music and his growing influence through the intermediary of the enlightened composers of the period had among the audiences of the salons.

CLUES

Marcel Proust, not so much in the way in which he encodes reality (combining for example several models to create a character, a place, or an episode of his novel, so true is it that fiction is more demanding than reality and needs always more material from which to extract an essence) as in the notes into which he sometimes jettisons his ballast, carefully opens a breach through which biographers could rush, letting slip at times a confidence, a key, such as this clue from *In Memory of Murdered Churches*, about his mechanic Agostinelli (one of the models for Albertine). He remarks: "I hardly anticipated when I wrote these lines that seven or eight years later this young man would ask to type up a book of mine, would learn aviation under the name of Marcel Swann (in which he had had in a friendly way associated my Christian name and the name of one of my characters), and would die at the age of 26, in an airplane accident offshore of Antibes."

This note's feeling of objective and somewhat distant news is another mask for the real grief that the author felt at the disappearance of his friend whose confinement, departure, and accidental death would serve as the framework for *The Prisoner.*

He seems to have had a premonition of this tragic end, since a few lines later, after having compared the detached manner in which his chauffeur held the wheel to that in which the saints of the churches they visited together held either the symbol recalling their profession or their art, if not the weapon by which they perished, he adds: "May the steering wheel of the young mechanic who drives me always remain the symbol of his talent rather than becoming a foreshadowing of his torment."

SLOW AND STEADY

The pastiches are a final attempt to dodge, to delay, the coming of that other self who will become the author of *In Search of Lost Time.* No doubt sensing the entry into the irreversible that this metamorphosis meant, already imitating his favorite authors with considerable skill, Marcel Proust aims not only to free himself from their possible influence but also, for the time being, to not yet be himself. Through pastiche, he learns also to imitate, to recreate the linguistic turns of office people or of the faubourg Saint-Germain. But the as-yet-unrecognized project of the *Search* needed this delay, this subterranean maturing, these back alleys, to strengthen itself, and so that a conception of the whole might join, pick up again, transform, and enhance the principle episodes and characters already contained in *Jean Santeuil, Contre Sainte-Beuve,* and various preliminary drafts.

THE OTHER SELF

The narrator, surprised to find his own self again rather than another after a leaden sleep ("that beneficial access to mental alienation"), the way you rediscover a name, a verse, a forgotten refrain.

He compares sleep to death, awakening to resurrection, wondering if one could conceive of the resurrection of the soul after death as a phenomenon of memory.

What he suggests, without saying so, is that the self that is found again as if inadvertently after sleep, is, itself, a phenomenon of memory, a composition, the work of a life.

POLYPHONY

The pastiches are not just an amusing hors d'oeuvre before the serious work, but are also an account of a method. In the *Search*, Proust surrenders to an original pastiche of each of his role models so as to form, by melting them into a single fictive entity, each of the characters of his novel. He imitates, he apes, not only their way of speaking, walking, and holding themselves, but also their speech, their ideas, their obsessions. And he immerses it all in a pastiche of Saint-Simon.

Like the characters of the *Ring Cycle* whose arrival onstage, or even their evocation in a scene in which they don't appear, is pointed out and intensified by the musical phrase that identifies them, as if preceded by their leitmotif, each character in the *Search* has their own style, each is seemingly the emblem of themselves, if not their own caricature.

"And as the demon of pastiche, and of not appearing old hat, alters the most natural and most certain figure of oneself, Françoise, borrowing the expression from her daughter's vocabulary, used to say that I was wacky," adds the narrator in passing. (He had asked Françoise to pack his bags so he can go away for a few days and space out his morning appearances on Madame de Guermantes' path, then immediately after, thinking better of it, to unpack them.)

RELIGION OF THE ALLERGY

Since my insomnia persists, I get up and again take up *Pastiches and Melanges.* What irony, I tell myself: he needed retrenchment from the world—illness and insomnia—to write a work that today is the classic example of what you promise yourself to read or reread when you've broken a leg. In *Filial Sentiments of a Parricide* I then read: "Should a 'low pressure system move toward the Balearic Islands,' as the papers say, should the ground start to tremble in Jamaica, then at the same moment, in Paris, the migraine sufferers, the rheumatics, the asthmatics, no doubt the mad also, have their crises, so fully are the high-strung from the most distant points of the universe bound together by a solidarity that they often might wish was less intimate."

The hope of finally finding sleep arrives with the first bird-songs, when it isn't yet day but nothing any longer seems able to prevent its arrival. (What an absurd thought!)

Postscript. And Fromentin before: "I was born, I grew, and I will live dependent on certain occult forces to whose actions I am subjected without acknowledging them or being able to define them. There exists between the barometer and I little secrets that I don't share, afraid of confessing my servitude and of humiliating in the presence of mere matter a human soul pretending to be free."

EUGÈNE FROMENTIN'S CAMELS

A curious destiny, that of the painter Fromentin: beginning with the Salon of 1849, he carved out a reputation for himself as an orientalist, which he forever continued scrupulously perfecting, as if he had wanted to demonstrate—to his family? to himself?—a professionalism that people had refused to recognize in him. And yet it is clear that the real Fromentin (the author of *Dominique*), a sensitive soul and perceptive psychologist, is fully revealed in the several portraits that he left, much more so than in the scenes borrowed from genre paintings: the halt in the desert or the Berber riders before the fortress.

A specialist in renunciations, a sort of Oblomov, who didn't know how to, or didn't want to, or couldn't, risk the irreversible swerve where each distinctiveness is taken into the momentum which exceeds it. *A Year in the Sahel* remains a travelogue, *Dominique* a regret, and *The Old Masters* an essay. The right jolt, war, or asthma attack, and the Sahel becomes Venice as seen through Ruskin, the essay becomes *Contre Sainte-Beuve*, *Dominique*, Charles Swann, and the same disillusionment, a monument.

"What is clearer to me is that I wanted to please myself, to be moved again by memories, to regain my youth as I was moving away from it, and to express in the form of a book a good part of myself—the best—which will never find a place in my paintings," wrote Fromentin in 1862 to George Sand, who had expressed an interest in the first chapters of *Dominique* when they appeared in the *Revue des Deux Mondes*. Fromentin was to dedicate his novel to her.

Some time later, in the house at Auteuil, Madame Proust read to the young, ill Marcel passages from *The Country Waif*. The doctor had prescribed medication to lower his fever and permit the boy to eat a little; his mother who was "always in the right" decided on his diet and gave him *only milk*. To each his own forbidden madeleine.

BACKSTORY

I imagine that it is extremely rare for a reader of *Jean Santeuil* not to have read, beforehand, *In Search of Lost Time*. *Jean Santeuil* is therefore nearly always read in the light of the *Search*, with full knowledge of the facts. Foundations, archeology. Like the discovery that a historic site, a castle, a church, has been constructed at the location of, and on the very ruins of, another castle, another church whose baptismal fonts themselves cover an ancient spring previously consecrated by the druids. Like how the sudden discovery of the meaning of a local family name or place name makes a word which until then would have seemed to us closed, arbitrary, and foreign, open up, light up, blossom, and give off a recognizable scent.

Jean Santeuil emanates the charm of the recognizable, relished by the music lover, who, as he hears a melody, hums it within. Charm of intensification, of rereading, augmented further if what is thus *reread* is nevertheless new.

"The supplemental lines that you are going to read aim only to reintroduce after the fact a bit of the awkward world that had served to fashion it back into the already shaking edifice of the poem" says René Char in his introduction to *L'Arrière-histoire du poème pulverisé.*

Of course, the words of *Jean Santeuil* don't aim at the same target, but they have the same effect, from which comes their strange power...

TO SIGNAL

The pleasure most listeners draw from music is the completely Proustian one of reminiscence. I'm speaking here of pure musical reminiscence and not of the varied memories that a melody can awaken. The reminiscence of a melodic line, of a tempo, of a timbre, of a tone of voice, of the hesitation or decisiveness of a touch. The pleasure of returning, when the train or car approaches a place from childhood, how the air seems suddenly lighter, the sky higher, the horizon larger, from the vague feeling that something is bound to occur, and then, at a bend in the road, in the fork an old tree, in the gable of a house, in the fence of a field, the past signals to us. Music intermittently throws us those sorts of signs that immerse us in bliss. "A sign is that which is repeated. Without repetition, no sign, because one wouldn't be able to recognize it, and recognition is what the sign is based on," says Roland Barthes.

TIME MACHINE[4]

Under the title *Grand Hotel,* André Hardellet tells the story of a dream that reminds me of the atmosphere of a Julien Gracq tale or a film by André Delvaux, *One Night... A Train.*

A train drops a traveler off on the quay of an empty and nameless station. The character goes into the small town and to a Belle-Epoque style hotel that evokes in his memory a book whose title he can't manage to recall.

This hotel is deserted, but everything is in place, as if the décor were drawn up for an imminent film shoot, as if, at the

---

4. *Time Machine* was the name of the boat on which, a few years ago and in the company of friends, we sailed up not the river of time but the Nile, which is almost the same thing. This boat, made out of wood, which it seemed had belonged to King Farouk, was the last to still move by paddlewheel: being therefore rather quiet, it was the only boat authorized to sail at night; each morning upon climbing up the passageway we discovered, with the rising sun, a new landscape, a sort of biblical postcard.

Barely underway, settled in the tiny cabin at water level, immediately going out again to *recollect* my bearings, I couldn't shake an impression of déjà vu, which I attributed to tiredness. I learned later that the boat had been the setting for the film *Death on the Nile,* adapted from a novel by Agatha Christie. The cabins, the passageways, the bridge, and finally the little lounge paneled in polished wood with coppery gleams had been the theater of the murky affair in which Hercule Poirot manages to expose the murderer after suspicion is placed in turn, as is proper, on each of the characters.

"clack" of the stage manager, a crowd of extras, head-waiters, bellboys and maids, must suddenly appear and bustle about doing all the small tasks which would stir up this place, dozing like Sleeping Beauty's castle.

"Then it's by finding the title of the book again that you will discover reality," Hardellet says, suddenly transformed into some sort of Hercule Poirot, a decipherer of riddles.

"Clearly someone is expected, but not you. You: he for whom all has been kept intact, inalterable within Lost Time. He who would alone be able to give life and meaning to this mausoleum again: the cautious, the fragile 'narrator' in search of his own reality, the athlete of the cork chamber."

"While waiting, you will have to figure things out as best you can: at the nameless station, on the tracks overrun by wild grasses, trains that might take you no longer come by," concludes Hardellet. Said in another way, you must find again, alone, the path from Proust to self, even if it means taking improvised shortcuts. This is what Hardellet does in this other story, which I would gladly subtitle: "Taking the Desires of Others for Realities."

Again, the scene takes place in a hotel, not far from the Champs-Élysées. A rebellion has taken hold of the city; armed bands have taken control of the principal buildings and in particular of the hotel where the narrator is found. From the lobby in which he stands he sees coming down the staircase "the most sumptuous of the chambermaids," who immediately offers herself to him. "Words flow on in my mind as if dictated: pute, pubis, obus, Putbus."[5]

"The Baroness Putbus' chambermaid—but of course!" as our Hercule Poirot of the moment, enlightened by this Leirisian glossary, would say.

---

5. Translator's note: This could be translated *"prostitute, pubis, bomb, Putbus"* but the closeness of the verbal play is lost.

CONTAGION

Jean Santeuil, Volume II: "because you had to drop a short distance from the entangled slopes, and then slide your way along the face of the enormous boulders…" Or how one text visits another, introducing itself into the other's duration, into its phrasing, into its articulations. Do you hear the diminished sounds of the model in this poor tracing of the first verses of *The Drunken Boat?*

A little earlier, we read, in the exact style of a primary school dictation: "The sole sound to be heard was the preening of the vain Virginia creeper." But the style is also the thought. Reading *Jean Santeuil* is to witness the emergence, slow here, lightning-quick there, of originality, of deviance, of proper genius wrested from the most conventional prevailing milieu there is.

THE POSTERITY OF THE MORTEMART WIT

From Louis, the Duke of Saint-Simon, Marcel Proust borrowed more than the famous Mortemart wit, that combination of energy, grace, and uniqueness in language, that art of "weaving a story on the spot." For Saint-Simon, the Mortemart wit is not a simple trait that the duke would have identified and isolated, like the way the scientist who isolates a virus is undeniably its discoverer. It's quite simply his poetic art, the spinal column of his *Memoirs.*

Saint-Simon treats the Mortemart wit favorably because he recognizes himself in it. For the same reason, Marcel Proust makes it the model for the Guermantes wit. The Mortemart wit gives shape to a fantasy.

But deep down it is from the *Memoirs,* taken as a whole, that Marcel Proust weaves a story on the spot. An ambitious man, cultivating a fussy formalism, punctilious like no other for the considerations that he esteems are owed to his rank, brings his social career to an end and devotes himself entirely to a great work: the transmutation of life into art. The subject of the *Search* is there, and its style is already an integral part of it. You steal with impunity only that in which you authentically recognize yourself.

Would another great Saint-Simonian have found his master-piece in the turn of a phrase?

"Alberoni was the son of a gardener, who, feeling clever, had taken the collar so that he could, as a priest, go places from which his smock would have excluded him."

Stendhal, the miserable bookworm, finds in these words *The Red and the Black*. The Mortemart wit has struck again!

Despite your telling me that a fact is a fact, even if incidental, and that the seminary was in Stendhal's time, as in Saint-Simon's, the only means for a poor boy to get an education, I maintain that the news item recounted by the *Gazette des Tribunaux* which inspired Stendhal—Berthet, a former seminarian shoots at Mme Michoud, the mother of the children he tutored and who was probably his mistress—is not enough to make a novel. It props it up, it is the framework for it, but not the content. No novel without a little of the Mortemart wit. The content is the turn of a phrase, its contagious charm and peculiarity, which spark, in a forty-seven year old man who has not yet written his great book, the desire that this time carries him to a masterpiece. His own ambition for a great book is what Stendhal recognizes in Alberoni's collar.

CLUES, AGAIN

Through a brilliant premonition, isn't it all the ambiguity of his own nature that the narrator projects into the double character of Charles Marie, intimate friend of M. Santeuil, parliament member, "former Minister of Finance who might again become such from one day to the next," of whom one learns that he is still embroiled in the most crooked affairs? How can a man at the height of his career have been crazy enough to compromise himself to this degree? But he's like everyone, or nearly, says the narrator, like the libertine who picks up a woman on the boulevard and isn't ignorant of the risks he lays himself open to, like the gourmand who despite knowing gout has its eye on him doesn't give up his glass of alcohol, like "the lazy man who doesn't write the book that shall make his name live on."

It's because, the narrator tells us, "possible fear is weak against certain pleasure. Already a force emanating from the arms of the woman, from an unexplored sea, from the canapé or the cigarette that detains us, from the stroll that appeals to us, starts to disrupt our brain and makes it quite appropriate to imagine the pleasure that, so near to us, already makes our heart beat faster; there's no way we'll sacrifice such opportunities of ephemeral pleasure, even at the risk of irreparable unhappiness. Also, every day we see the pleasure seekers looking everywhere for pleasure, the travelers traveling, the lazy lazing around, and the living enjoying life one day at a time without thinking of death."

And in the opinion of Madame Marie commending her former minister husband to the Santeuils on her deathbed: "If he ever does wrong, it can only be that his kind heart has been led astray by those who didn't deserve him." An opinion which the narrator doubts was always as assured as the one which was then shared by the Santeuils and, along with them, the whole *classe politique* ("who will ever know to what uncertain and vagrant degree extreme blindness is mixed, in profound affection, with extreme clear-sightedness?"). Aren't we already seeing the slightly transposed image of the author's idea of the uncertain opinion his mother has of him?

Already feeling in himself what his education calls the forces of evil, debauchery, and laziness, to doubt that his mother had noticed these tendencies even before they had shown themselves would be to doubt her love itself and to hypothesize in its place what he most feared: indifference.

To insinuate the description of Charles Marie's character with the appropriate comparisons, to hint that the deputy's dying wife might have doubted the integrity of her husband, is for the narrator to leave a trail for those who know how to read it, a clue by which to return to the concept—completely fictive—of *true nature.*

In the way the born criminal (concerned at once with hiding his act and of nevertheless not making the discovery of his crimes and the punishment that deep down he seeks henceforth impossible) leaves in plain sight, but encoded, the evidence that condemns him, the author—a sort of Tom Thumb who awakens from the fabulous world of childhood only to dive into that no less confused world of fiction—leaves behind him in the weft of his sentence the bread crumbs that biographers, or simply admirers, feed on. Because the trap functions wonderfully, only those who have paid the tribute, who have desired, read, loved, *made his name live*, will have a right to the truth. Said in another way, only attentive readers, those whom love will have forgiven in advance, as a mother would do, will have the right to the confession of our depravity.

And Charles Marie? It is with merciless skill that Proust finishes off, at the same time as his chapter, this worn character. Having endured scandals and dishonor, the deputy who is forced to resign withdraws under general contempt, then: "The public's rage grew tired. His *Memoirs* were accepted for publication by the *Revue des Deux Mondes*. In moments of crisis, the newspapers of the opposition interviewed him once or twice. He was asked to preside at a banquet for the schoolteachers of his region. On the way home, he caught a cold, and died two days later of pneumonia."

SHADOWS

Lourdes Castro, the painter, primarily draws shadows or silhouettes: she attempts to harness the marks that permit identification by limiting herself to the outline, and not necessarily from its most easily recognizable angle.

At the request of an American magazine, she drew, superimposed on one another, the silhouettes of Samuel Beckett and Marcel Proust. The two photographic portraits from which she drew her inspiration are famous; Proust's head is leaning to the right, his chin is resting on his hand, that of Beckett is inclined to the left, and I believe I remember that in this photograph he wears a turtleneck sweater. Proust's silhouette seems to emanate from Beckett's as if his soul, his shadow, his continuation.

The artist notes in the margin: "I noticed during the drawing of their silhouettes that the outline of one is soft and round, while that of the other is stiff and angular."

She adds: "Each time I take up one of Beckett's works I savor the density of something infinitely reduced and I think of shadows, which are in fact the very simple portrait of someone's fundamental characteristics."

Shadows, those produced on the wall of the narrator's childhood room by the magic lantern projecting the legend of Geneviève de Brabant.

Satie composed stage music for a shadow puppet version of this legend.

TO FINISH OR NOT, AGAIN

From the endless accumulation of indexes which combine to demonstrate, reinforce, deepen, and open up an intuition, an initial suspicion, which becomes little by little the lesson of the whole work, Proust's undertaking poses in an exemplary manner the question of completion.

And of its ambiguity.

Exemplary because it doesn't avoid ambiguity; on the contrary, that's what it's based on.

"My work is finished," Samuel Beckett responds to the person who asked him (October 1987) what he was writing. And you know what courage, what lucidity, what high ambition, what moral sense, what athlete's discipline will have led the work of saint Samuel Beckett to this point where it is possible to say, without bitterness, without snobbery: my work is finished. To never repeat, to be as concise as possible, to tighten form endlessly, to stamp out overindulgence, to flee from tested formulations, to undermine one's own territory so that it's impossible to return to it, to burn his boats, to never stop confronting silence with his screaming and screaming. What a catechism!

In every coherent body of work there is a story, a weft, a thread, which connects isolated books and draws a sort of biography of their author, a portrait reduced to the essentials, at once blurred and astonishingly precise, like those silhouettes that Lourdes Castro draws.

This bird's-eye view, which unifies disparate points to make concluding a major trope in Robert Musil, Samuel Beckett, Michel Leiris, Edmond Jabès, Louis-René des Forêts, Roger Laporte, Claude Royet-Journoud, Roger Lewinter.

Musil, we've already seen.

Beckett, seen, said, even if ill-seen, ill-said. The nearly-final words stammered three times are: *afaint afar away over there what.*

Leiris, or how to drag things out without betrayal, the rules of the game having magnified the age of man, how to increase dignity through an excess of contrition, the body of work ends with these snapshots in hard pencil: *Ondes (Waves)* and *Images de marque (Brand Images)* by which the author, following the example of his brother Giacometti, continues to alter his portrait with negating strokes and alterations.

Jabès: I remember my and Jacques Dupin's stupefaction when speaking to Edmond Jabès in a more or less social gathering, with us enquiring about his health, his work, when he told us that he had started a new cycle. *The Book of Questions* seemed to us not to be able to—not to have to—finish, a book nevertheless always on the point of stopping, but without concluding, in peril with each line, seeming ready to fail rather than to finish.

Des Forêts: the strange and haunting adventure of *Ostinato,* fragments of a whole which doesn't exist, each fragment a perfect pearl from a non-existent necklace, competing with what came before, but not permitting a narrative which would reclaim its collapse; a pure amorous reiteration that fears more than anything to reach its ending. (Parenthetically, has someone pointed out the deliberately anti-Proustian title—therefore controlled by Proust, as if terrified of Proust—under which des Forêts published the fragments of *Ostinato: Facing the Immemorable*.)

Laporte: "Pursuit, demand without limits, has formed a pact with the end to the very degree in which it is always lacking," but the author remarks that this end isn't separated by an infinite number of sequences; the sixth sequence of *Moriendo*, the last of the nine books that compose *A Life*, is very much the last, or rather the penultimate one: it is followed with the lone word *continue*, which was the first word of the first sequence, a word that alone, on a white page, could claim to be the title of the sequence. In a postscript which gives the sixth sequence the status of being the penultimate, we discover the last word of the story, between quotation marks like a citation or a magic formula: "The final sequence will remain unwritten."

Claude Royet-Journoud has devoted his life to the luminous articulations that in some thirty years have ended up providing the material for four slim volumes, salvaged from an enormous mass of prose produced daily, from which he extracts a few splinters hard as diamonds. Since the appearance of *Les Natures indivisibles*, the tetralogy that he has always claimed to be working on is now standing on all four of its feet. It doesn't have a title, only the four parts do, which makes it so that nothing in advance would stand in the way of, at the appearance of a fifth volume, the author declaring that he always intended to work toward a pentalogy, then a sextet, a heptalogy. But no, Claude Royet-Journoud is not this sort of man; he says what he thinks, and when he thinks it he does it. So then, everyone wonders what life will be, for him, for you, for me, after the word END alone on a page, like Laporte's *continue.* "The temptation is strong to stick to it," he answers, and he confesses his affection for authors of just one book. There are many ways of being the author of a single book: to have a military career and publish *Dangerous Liaisons,* to be an acclaimed orientalist painter and write *Dominique,* to endlessly rework the same collection of poems, like Gilbert Lély, to make *Contre Saint-Beuve* and *Jean Santeuil* the rough drafts of the *Search,* to sink into the labyrinths of the *other state.*

With *The Appeal of Things,* Roger Lewinter, editor of Diderot, translator of Groddeck, Karl Kraus, and the most beautiful version in French of the *Duino Elegies,* gave us a book stretched to the limit. From some autobiographical givens—Groddeck, the illness and death of his father, the impassioned search in the flea market for old opera recordings, love, and solitude—Lewinter created a melody that was sinuous, secret, haunting and, finally, dazzling. With *who—in the order—to the evening redness— words* he's now publishing the outline of a rather strange adventure. It is five dense pages without an opening capital or closing period, followed by an insert that reproduces the same five pages in a slightly different version. The fanatical care with which each displacement, each inversion is brought about in the most perfect control of its effects—effects of meaning—indicates that we find ourselves, here more often than before, at the heart of the question of writing: within the syntax. Thus always, from version to version, sinking into greater strictness, obscure, luminous. For more than ten years, Lewinter has worked at modifying, by successive numbered versions, the first four pages of a story that should initially have amounted to twenty pages. With more or less the same narrative elements as in *The Appeal of Things* and an implacable logical rigorousness, he produces a strange and captivating prose that comes undone at the same time as it is constructed by multiplication and segmentation of interpolated clauses, so that the principal proposition is always in some way still to come. We find ourselves seemingly dangling in the totality of the language that is virtually at our disposal, carried away in a movement of excitement whose conclusion will be always deferred. Not yet, not right away, Lewinter says implicitly.

There is in all these bodies of work a fierce, stubborn will to speak that is matched only by a fierce and stubborn will to fall silent.

UNIVERSAL RESTITUTION

For the price of a rather simple calculation, starting from the number of letters of the alphabet and the average length of words in the language, you can establish the possible number of words. This number is finite. And it even includes all the words which mean nothing.

Based on the average number of words in a line, of lines on a page, and of pages in a volume, it is possible to state the number, also finite, of all possible books. (It will include all the books that don't mean anything and even all those that, while perfectly possible, will never see the light of day.) In other words, the number of all possible books, written with words that are real and more or less signify something, is much smaller than the number that Leibniz calculated, based, for the convenience of the calculation, upon an alphabet of 100 letters: 1 followed by 7,300,000,000,000 zeros. These books potentially contain, he says, all pronounceable or unpronounceable truths or falsehoods. It follows that all individual stories, all the events of everyone's lives, which are the material of diaries or of autobiographies that could be written if they insisted on keeping track, are contained in this number. From which it follows that, if humanity lasts long enough, we will be sure to arrive at the moment when

"Nullum est jam dictum, quod non dictum sit prius"[6] (Leibniz is citing Terence).

That's how in 1693 Gottfried Wilhelm Leibniz imagines what he calls *Apocatastasis* or *palingenesis* or *universal restitution*: the number of individual stories being finite, there will necessarily come a moment when they will have to repeat themselves: "Myself, for example, living in a city called Hanover, situated on the banks of the Leine, occupied with the History of Brunswick, writing to the same friends letters having the same meaning," he says.

If he didn't know this fable worthy of Borges (in which, incidentally, the man from Hanover was a firm believer, to the point of writing to Fontenelle to have it communicated to the French Academy), either Roger Lewinter sensed it, or it was unconsciously *restituted*. Thus we see him moving words like Archimedes moving grains of sand from Syracuse into the Pythagorean orb.

Completion, incompletion, the infinite in the finite, the number of grains of sand. All the works of which I have just spoken are works that double, that are their own mirror, that must in principle be reread. Like *The Odyssey*, like *Don Quixote*, like *The Count of Monte Cristo*. (A few weeks before his death, Michel Leiris read for the first time *The Count of Monte Cristo* and was amazed that he had postponed for so long that moment, which

---

6. Translator's note: Nothing is said that hasn't been said before.

he enjoyed with a jubilation that his natural reserve could not conceal.) Works which reread themselves, which rewrite themselves, works whose writing is at every moment a rereading and a rewriting. Quixotism, recalls Claude Levi-Strauss, is not the mania for righting wrongs, for making oneself the champion of the oppressed, or for climbing aboard lost causes; it is "an obsessive desire to find the past behind the present." "The present is pregnant with the future," says Leibniz again. And Spinoza: "The instant contains eternity." And Claude Royet-Journoud: "What comes prior is what follows."

DELTA

Proust is everywhere. That's what genius is. Shakespeare
and a few others. The few about whom one can say, along with
Borges, that "they are like all other men except in this: that they
are like all other men." Leibniz, him again, used the word *dig-
nity* where we commonly use the term *power*. To elevate to the
second, tenth, nth dignity ... Well, these men, the small number
of those who are like Borges's Shakespeare, are elevated to the
x dignity, x being the number of all other men, past, present
and future. The number of grains of sand. A pair of glasses; you
have read them, and every time you rediscover them, you find
yourself with that pair of glasses on your nose. Can you see a
haystack, a row of poplars, without thinking of Monet, an apple
without thinking of Cézanne?

Today it is in Joë Bousquet that I hear Proust. A letter to
Francine, dated July 1928. They have quarreled, she has taken
back her letters, he is upset with her, from his bed he raises his
eyes toward the flowers that she brought him, and he writes:
"They live, and my happiness from seeing them in your hands
survives with them. Deaf to our quarrel, their colors burned this
whole evening before us with love." And suddenly it is Proust
who is speaking: "They are like those corners of our soul that
bad news doesn't reach, and that continue to be delighted by a

happiness that won't return."

And again here: "When I see the beach of Biarritz in 1931 (Lartigue) or the Pont des Arts in 1932 (Kertész) I tell myself: 'Perhaps I was there; perhaps that's me among the swimmers or the passersby, one of those summer afternoons when I took the Bayonne tramway to go swimming on the *Grande Plage*, or one of those Sunday mornings when, coming from our apartment on the Rue Jacques-Callot, I crossed the bridge to go to the Temple de l'Oratoire...'" (Roland Barthes: *Camera Lucida*). Did you hear? *One of those Sunday mornings when, coming from our apartment*. No doubt, he is there. Has Proust shaped our perception to such a degree that it is no longer possible to evoke with a word a snippet of the personal past without, even just in the placement of a comma, Proustian music ringing out like a signal of recognition? A familiar tune, the auditory equivalent of déjà vu.

In *Camera Lucida*, Proust's name takes a long time to appear. The author's mother does too. The entire first part, the first hundred pages, endeavors not to stray from semiology. Barthes, even if he readily uses the first person singular, retains, if not the pompous tone of the professor, at least the more intimate one of the researcher.

But at the beginning of the second part, he cracks. Letting go, he brings together in the same sentence Proust, the death of his mother, and photography. And in so doing he initiates a story. The story until then delayed. As if the death of his mother had encouraged a latent identification with Proust. As if the barricade of academic discourse had given way and the story was finally possible. "With her dead, I no longer have any reason to march in step with the progress of the superior life force (the species). My particularity could never again universalize itself (except utopically, through writing, whose project, from then on, would become the sole goal of my life)."

The past (the very nature of the photographed), the death of the mother, and even the project of writing a book. The project of writing a book is more alive than the book itself; it is of desire. In 1968, Barthes pointed out that the Proustian narrator is not the person who has seen or felt, nor even the person who writes, but rather he who is going to write. All was in place for a great novel haunted by a great model. But Barthes, disconsolate and acting like a widower, chose to let himself be knocked down by a car, and to not heal from it.

In *Camera Lucida*, the photograph which illustrates the part of his book in which he speaks for the first time of his mother is a portrait of Ernestine Nadar taken by Félix Nadar, and the ambiguous caption of the photograph indicates "mother or wife of the artist."

Although photography is pure contingency ("it is always something which is represented" says Barthes), the text takes, as soon as it wants to, its revenge, and, as it's a matter of identifying the *something*, ambiguity is born again through the caption.

"The mediator of a truth, the same as Nadar making out of his mother (or of his wife, no one knows) one of the most beautiful photographs in the world" that's how Barthes sees "the obscure photographer of Chennvières sur Marne" who had taken the snapshot of the little girl in the Winter Garden in which he finally found his mother again. "For once," he says, "photography gave me a feeling as certain as memory, such as Proust experienced, when, bending down one day to take off his shoes he abruptly recovered from his memory the face of his true grandmother." Grandmother of the narrator but mother of the author.

Why was the same photograph by Nadar used by the editor to illustrate the cover of the French translation of *Maria Grubbe* by Jens Peter Jacobsen? I don't know. I only know that this fact helps to tighten the secret weft that links some of the subtle realities by which life is sometimes elevated to the status of fiction.

Intrigued first of all by an admiring mention that Roger Caillois had made of him, then, immediately after, by the praises that Rilke bestows on him in the *Letters to a Young Poet*, I had for years looked to obtain Jacobsen's most lauded novel and the only one then translated into French, *Niels Lyhne*, which had appeared in the 30s and hadn't been reprinted since.

In Copenhagen, where its status as a great classic wasn't enough to keep it in the windows of the bookstores, I had found nevertheless a nice old edition, but in Danish, which fulfilled my impulse toward fetishism but didn't move me forward a great deal along the path to knowledge. It was again out of fetishism that at Oslo, near to the port, I acquired nearly all the books of Knut Hamsun in their original version, simply because their titles fired my imagination: *Men livet lever, Segelfoss by, Landstrykere, Markens grode, Svaernere, Paa gjengrodde stier, Under hoststjaernen,* and the famous *Sult.* I still have them and, in my rather disorganized library, I found them instantly so as to recopy the titles here with the feeling of accomplishing a little ritual of contemplation. In the end, they mean more to me today than the French translations in which I read them and that I have now consigned to storage. It's perhaps because the spirit of Knut Hamsun is for me more present in these mute little books... That's how ghosts are, they need very little to take up residence; an old book written in an unknown language can do the trick, and the face of the old fascist jerk, part-colonel from La Roque and part-Noël Roquevert, of the nonagenarian Knut Hamsun as a grumpy warrant officer has never succeeded in erasing the tenderness that I feel for the young fanciful man of *Sult.*

Niels Lyhne. The death of the mother is the central episode and the culminating point of this fine book, constantly quivering with suppressed effusiveness. A short time after reading it, I gave it to Michel Leiris (we had gotten into the habit during each of my visits of exchanging something) because I thought its principal theme—what is poetry and how to preserve the flame of it in a world which overlooks it—would appeal to him, since he continued with admirable determination to explore this infinite subject, which is, by nature, evasive, and collects pure crystals wrenched from the void as a jealous lover collects signs of infidelity.

But to *Niels Lyhne* (*"ou ce nihil inné (or this nihilo innate)*)" as he had written when signing my copy of *Langage Tangage*, adding thus, which was to me a gift in return, a new gloss to his old glossary) Leiris still preferred *Maria Grubbe*, or the blossoming into degeneration—a character who also captivated Robert Musil, who in his journal described her as "a beautiful arabesque, frail as a flower, but often extravagant, baroque."

Was it that same day or another that Michel Leiris declared that he found admirable in all points the first pages of *Ostinato*, with which Louis-René des Forêts had broken, in the *Nouvelle Revue Française*, a long silence that those of his admirers who, like me, weren't aware of what new adventure he had thrown himself, had feared was definitive.

I like the fact that at the end of this short work in which leniency has been the rule the names of Proust, Jacobsen, Hardellet, Caillois, Musil, Leiris, Beckett, des Forêts, Barthes, Laporte, Royet-Journoud, and Lewinter have joined in an affective constellation. Just like in the album in which William Howard Adams brought together the majority of the people from which Proust must have drawn his inspiration. The evocation of their names alone—Charles Haas, Marie de Benardaky, Boni de Castellane, Robert de Montesquiou, the Prince Boson de Sagan, Laure Hayman—is enough to make them come back to life in a moment: something of their souls has been forever captured and continues to nourish the immortal character which developed from this graft. But we also find in this album Monet, Fauré,

Debussy, Anatole France, and Reynaldo Hahn, all photographed by Nadar, no longer Félix, but his son Paul who, starting in 1880, took over management of the famous studio where his father organized the first Impressionist exhibition.

Real people or fictional characters, both for me are faces in a game, face cards whose values surpass that of the number cards. And what's more, they're doubled, mirrored along a diagonal axis (that Roger Caillois would have loved) held in a single hand, hidden hand, hand declared, trump takes all.

Not having found a vacant room in the city, I went into exile on the Lido, seated in the back of a *vaporetto*, Mahler in my head like a musical postcard; then I crossed the island, deserted at the hour of the siesta, slowing down my pace as if to calm a growing impatience, and entered after a few steps *under the moldings of pale green stucco.* A quick wash, and I went out, into the murmur of the high trees, down the path toward the tennis courts; I was alone and didn't meet anyone, but what I was looking for either wasn't there or, like the small green lizard which freezes a moment on the low wall, looks at me with an eye (it really is only the eye that moves to look at you, and nothing of the head nor the body) then disappears into a crack between two dry stones, had fled at my approach, had taken refuge in the wings, the service quarters, the surroundings of this theater of shadows visited by all the bit players of the painting that I was mentally reconstructing in the manner of the simulacra that Pierre Klossowski draws, in which one sees Sade, Freud, Bataille, Foucault, and several others joined.

I mused on the photograph that Louis-René des Forêts placed at end of the lovely dream story *Unhappiness on the Lido*: the portrait of Pierre Klossowski in a sailor suit, the same age as Tadzio.

Examination of alibis in the salon of the *Time Machine*, the hour come for accountability in the house at Auteuil, fancy-dress ball at the home of the Prince of Guermantes where the masks, in falling, uncover other masks?

Finally I left the Hotel des Bains, approached the Giardini, went along the Shore of Seven Martyrs, passed before the Danieli where you might have thought you saw Madame Proust's black shawl floating; I had the *Book of Disquiet* in my hand and I read: "To cease, to end at last, but surviving as something else: the page of a book, a tuft of disheveled hair, the quiver of the creeping plant next to the half-open window, the irrelevant footsteps in the gravel of the bend, the last smoke to rise from the village going to sleep, the wagoner's whip left on the early morning roadside..."[7]

The Traveler's Joy the English call the climbing viburnum because its presence on the hedges lining a road signals that you are approaching a hamlet. In dreams, in books, in pieces of music, in paintings, in the beings that we love, as on hiking trails,

---

7.   Fernando Pessoa, *The Book of Disquiet*, Richard Zenith, trans. (New York: Penguin, 2002), 32-33.

there are sometimes, scattered, signs of gratitude such as com-
pose the traveler's joy. They are fleeting, like sand, unstable,
like sand can be, innumerable… They attest to the presence of
something else, as do the shadows that reveal what's in the light,
as do the efforts of the dead who haunt the living.

The La Presse list:

1. *Theory of Prepositions*
by Claude Royet-Journoud
translated by Keith Waldrop

2. *Wolftrot*
by Marie Borel
translated by Sarah Riggs & Omar Berrada

3. *Heliotropes*
by Ryoko Sekiguchi
translated by Sarah O'Brien

4. *Exchanges on Light*
by Jacques Roubaud
translated by Eleni Sikelianos

5. *It*
by Dominique Fourcade
translated by Peter Consenstein

6. *Conditions of Light*
by Emmanuel Hocquard
translated by Jean-Jacques Poucel

7. *The Whole of Poetry is Preposition*
by Claude Royet-Journoud
translated by Keith Waldrop

www.lapressepoetry.com

This is the fifteenth title in the La Presse series of contemporary French poetry in English translation. The cover image is from the translator's first draft. The text is set in Bell with titles in Sukhumvit Set. The series is edited by Cole Swensen; the book was designed by Erica Mena, and the cover by Shari DeGraw.